OUR FA
FORGI
US - 1

Now I want to pray for
(tell God what you want to pray for)

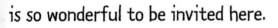

is so wonderful to be invited here.

od you are so good and kind.

am sorry that I am not always
ood and kind so we tell God.

5

OUR FATHER FORGIVES US - 2

Dear Father in heaven, thank you for your wonderful merciful love. I am glad you forgive me when I

(Tell God something you're sorry about)

GOD IS SO WONDERFUL

When Jesus was born the angels sang this song. We all join in happily. In Advent and Lent this prayer is left out as these are very serious times.

Glory to God in the highest,
and peace to his people on earth.
Lord God, heavenly King,
almighty God and Father,
we worship you,
we give you thanks,
we praise you for your glory.
Lord Jesus Christ, only Son of the Father,
Lord God, Lamb of God,
you take away the sin of the world:
have mercy on us;
you are seated at the right hand of the Father:
receive our prayer.
For you alone are the Holy One,
You alone are the Lord,
You alone are the Most High,
Jesus Christ,
with the Holy Spirit,
in the glory of God the Father.
Amen.

I will draw or write something I have seen or heard this week that makes me want to praise and thank God.

WE LISTEN TO GOD'S WORD -1

I listen to people who are important to me.
I listen to things I like.
So I will listen to the Word of God.

The First Reading

Before Jesus was born God spoke to people through holy men and women. God told the people to be kind to the poor and to strangers because God was kind to everyone.
Above all, God promised to send Jesus.

Today the first reading is about…

The Second Reading

After Jesus had gone back to heaven his friends wrote letters about him. The letters remind us how wonderful Jesus was. Sometimes they say we are the brothers and sisters of Jesus, so we can be like Jesus too.

Today the second reading is about…

Each reading ends with the words:
This is the word of the Lord

WE SAY:
Thanks be to God.

WE LISTEN TO GOD'S WORD -2

It is always exciting to hear good news.
The Gospel is the Good News which God gives us.
It is all about Jesus.

Sometimes it is a story that Jesus told us. Sometimes it is something that Jesus did. We stand up when we hear the Good News and we welcome the Gospel. Alleluia.

Dear Father in heaven, I will listen carefully to the Gospel.
Thank you for the Good News.

THE PRIEST INTRODUCES:

> The Gospel of Our Lord Jesus Christ according to (Matthew, Mark, Luke or John).

Today's Gospel is about⋯

WE HEAR MORE ★ ★ ABOUT THE READINGS

Sermon ★ ☆ ★

We sit while the priest talks about the readings.
If the priest is talking to the children I will listen carefully.
If he is talking to grown-ups I can choose what to do.

1 I could listen and try to understand.

2 I could think about the Gospel and imagine that I was there. What would I say to Jesus? What would he say to me?

3 I could tell God in my heart that I want to understand. I will keep saying in my heart, very very slowly, 'Speak Lord, I am listening.'

God is speaking to me in the readings and the sermon. When I leave Church I will try to remember this message from God all through the week.

DRAW A PICTURE OF THE GOSPEL

WE BELIEVE IN GOD AND THE CHURCH

We stand to proclaim our faith.

We believe in one God, the Father, the Almighty,
maker of heaven and earth,
of all that is, seen and unseen.
　　We believe in one Lord, Jesus Christ,
　　the only Son of God,
　　eternally begotten of the Father,
God from God, Light from Light,
true God from true God,
begotten, not made,
of one Being with the Father,
through him all things were made.
　　For us and for our salvation he came down from heaven:
　　was incarnate from the Holy Spirit
　　and the Virgin Mary and was made man.
For our sake he was crucified under Pontius Pilate;
he suffered death and was buried.
　　On the third day he rose again
　　in accordance with the Scriptures:
　　he ascended into heaven
　　and is seated at the right hand of the Father:
He will come again in glory to judge the living and the dead,
and his kingdom will have no end.
　　We believe in the Holy Spirit,
　　the Lord, the giver of life,
　　who proceeds from the Father and the Son,
　　who with the Father and the Son is worshipped and glorified,
　　who has spoken through the Prophets.
We believe in one, holy, catholic and apostolic Church.
We acknowledge one baptism for the forgiveness of sins.
We look for the resurrection of the dead, and the life of the world to come.
　　　　　　　　　　　　Amen.

WE PRAY FOR THE WHOLE WORLD

Bidding Prayers

Jesus tells us that God always listens to our prayers and gives us what is good for us.

I will pray for people in the church.
I will pray for people in other countries.
I will pray for people who help me.
I will pray for people who are poor or sad.
I will pray for myself.

Write down the names of people who need your prayers. If you can help them during the week write down what you can do for them.

O Lord hear my prayer

13

A SIGN OF PEACE

We have listened to the word of God.
We have heard the Good News in the gospel.
We have prayed for other people and ourselves
now the priest invites us to share the
peace of the Lord with those around us.

THE PRIEST SAYS:

The peace of the Lord be always with you.

WE SAY:
and also with you.

THE PRIEST SAYS:

Let us offer one another a sign of peace.

We give a loving sign, a kiss or a handshake to show
that we are all part of God's family.

WE BRING THE GIFTS TO THE ALTAR

We bring the bread, the wine and the money to the altar.
We need food, drink and money to stay alive.
We bring our lives to the altar.

I offer you the hardest work I did this week. It was…

I offer you the happiest time I had this week. It was…

I offer you my sad times as well.
Help me to be brave.

THE EUCHARISTIC PRAYER

This is the special moment of the service.
The gifts of bread and wine have been placed on the altar.

THE PRIEST SAYS:
The Lord be with you.

WE SAY:
And also with you.

Now the Eucharistic prayer is said
by the priest alone. It may be
different each week but always
includes:
praise to God for his mighty acts
a reminder of what happened at
the Last Supper and what Jesus'
death on the cross means to us.
Then the priest asks the Holy Spirit
to be with us all.
We join in silently and listen
carefully to hear each part of the
prayer.

GOD'S POWER AND MIGHT

Preface

The priest says a prayer of praise and thanks to God. This prayer changes at different times of the year. At Christmas the priest thanks God for sharing our life when he became a human being. At Easter he thanks God for the gift of everlasting life which Jesus gave us by his death and resurrection.

At this Holy Communion I praise and thank God for...

THE GIFTS BECOME JESUS OUR FOOD OF LIFE

The priest remembers what Jesus said and did at his Last Supper. He says and does the same.

JESUS SAID: Take
Eat
Take
Drink.

THE PRIEST SAYS: Take
Eat
Take
Drink.

18

WE SHOW OUR BELIEF

As the priest says the words I will look up at the bread. It is now the Bread of Life. Then I will look up at the wine. It is now the Cup of Salvation.

This is me. I give you my life.

As I gave myself for you on the cross.

This is the great mystery which we believe in. To show our belief we say one of these prayers.

The priest continues the prayers and asks the Holy Spirit to be with us and help us to praise God for ever.

I have joined my prayers with the prayers of the priest and everyone who is present.

WE GET READY TO RECEIVE JESUS -1

We stand and say the Our Father with everyo
We are all in God's family.

Our Father in heaven,
 hallowed be your name,
your kingdom come,
your will be done,
on earth as in heaven.
Give us today our daily bread.
Forgive us our sins
as we forgive those who sin against us.
Lead us not into temptation
but deliver us from evil.
For the kingdom, the power,
and the glory are yours
now and for ever.
Amen.

The priest then breaks the bread. . .